Rocks, Roads, Reflections

Rocks, Roads, Reflections

A Faith Journey

Shirley Biggerstaff Wright

FOREWORD BY
Robin Dease

RESOURCE *Publications* · Eugene, Oregon

ROCKS, ROADS, REFLECTIONS
A Faith Journey

Resource Publications
An Imprint of Wipf and Stock Publishers
199 W. 8th Ave., Suite 3
Eugene, OR 97401

www.wipfandstock.com

PAPERBACK ISBN: 979-8-3852-6996-9
HARDCOVER ISBN: 979-8-3852-6997-6
EBOOK ISBN: 979-8-3852-6998-3

VERSION NUMBER 01/07/26

Dedicated to

those who have walked the journey of faith alongside me,

especially my husband, Ken; my children:
Jonathan, Devi, and Melanie;

their spouses, and our beloved grandchildren.

Contents

Foreword

In the life of the pastor, words have always been more than ink on a page. They are breath, prayer, and testimony. They are the vessels through which God's Spirit stirs courage, heals wounds, and awakens hope. In this collection of poems, we are invited into the sacred imagination of a clergywoman whose voice rises from the pulpit, the pew, and the margins alike.

I have always been intrigued and perplexed by poetry. Poetry resists easy explanation; yet, it draws us in with its rhythm, imagery, and mystery. It paints pictures in the minds, opening doors to new ways of seeing reality. And a single line can pierce the heart, echoing experiences we did not know how to name.

Shirley's poetry is not ornamental; it is incarnational. You will discover God, love, faith and perseverance, forgiveness, leadership, vulnerability, sadness, loss, pain, redemption, and empowerment. These poems remind us that the Word became flesh not only in Bethlehem long ago but also in the lives of those who pour themselves out in service today.

I have seen how the Spirit equips clergywomen to speak truth with tenderness, to embody justice with grace, and to carry the gospel into places where silence once reigned. This collection is a continuation of that witness. It is both balm and provocation and comfort for the weary.

I commend these poems to you not only as literature but as liturgy. Read them aloud. Pray them in the quiet of your study. Share them in circles of trust. Let them remind you that ministry is poetry in motion, and that the church is at its best when it listens to voices that too often have been overlooked.

May you find in these pages the courage to rejoice, the strength to lament, and the vision to hope. And may the Spirit that inspired these words inspire all of us to walk more faithfully in the way of Christ.

—Bishop Robin Dease
  The United Methodist Church

Introduction

They make their entrance, floating as if a feather caught in a breeze—memories, that is. Here I am—filling the dishwasher, arranging Sunday's music, or pulling pesky weeds—and they land in my brain as if I had bidden them come.

Maybe it's a process of aging, a seventy-plus-year-old brain storing pictures much like the hard drive on my computer. Sometimes they are funny things like the mother duck marching her ducklings across the road as if she owned the section of highway whose traffic—like it or not—must pause so that they might get to the lake on the other side. Sometimes they are stories told by someone some time ago, the events so early in life that there is no tangible memory of having been there. But I was there—there sitting on my mother's lap, my brother beside her on the church pew, embarrassing her with his much-too-loud-for-church voice demanding, "Why is that woman's hair blue?" Other times, there are memories of frustrations prompted by Christmas decorations taken from their attic storage, only to discover chips or broken staves or fallen stars in the nativity set the grandchildren have come to love. As the season of Lent rolls around, memories of forehead smudges turned askew or wooden crosses posted at sidewalk's edge most certainly make their entrance from my "hard drive storage" and into conversations with friends around the dinner table. These and so many other life experiences give way to "Reflections," found in the final chapter of this book.

Oftentimes, the memories that crop up are concrete things like mountains, "rocks," popping up in the distance. Whether they be Stone Mountain soaring on the horizon as I travel south on I-85 from my home, or Chimney Rock, part of the Blue Ridge always visible from my childhood home, they are metaphors for strength and support, the firm foundation on which to build—in this case, to establish lives of faith.

But besides these literal rocks, there are the symbolic rocks in our lives of faith—the people who have encouraged us to begin the journey in faith or who have supported us when faith seemed to escape us. Parents, grandparents, Sunday School teachers, pastors—these "rocks" are different for all of us, but chances are, from time to time, a memory of one of them comes unbidden from our hard drive brains. If we are lucky, that memory comes at a time that provides ample space to simply revel in the joy that accompanies it, and even more importantly, opportunities to give thanks. The first section of this collection, "Rocks" may just provide a memory nudge, and one of these "rocks" in your experience may come flying in like a feather on a breeze.

Besides rocks, roads sometimes are symbols for our journeys in faith. The road metaphor may prove adequate to describe some of the difficulties, challenges, and losses that are a part of life. The road up Saluda Grade in North Carolina, with its twists and turns, narrow shoulders, and its impossible-to-see-the-ground-down-below serves well in this regard. Perhaps more fitting, however, for your own particular life challenges is the Tail of the Dragon. Negotiating a U-shaped turn, ready to give thanks for having maneuvered it, only to discover the next U-shaped turn and then another and then another, speaks to difficulties that sometimes occur rapid-fire in life. It would be a disservice to fail to acknowledge the challenges that are a part of any journey in faith, but it would also be a disservice to fail to pause and give thanks for all the beautiful experiences along the way as well. On roads such as the ones my husband and I often travel in North Georgia, we are amazed at the beauty: the orange and red leaves of fall, or the pink hues in groves of mountain laurel, or dense patches of ferns along the forest edges. In any event, the title, "Roads" as it applies to the second section of the book, invites readers into this specific metaphor for the life of faith. Indeed, while "Roads" help us acknowledge the difficulties and challenges, they sometimes are the very "therapy" that we need as we soak in the beauty of God's creation. May we always be eternally grateful to God, the "Rock" of our Salvation, the God whose road always leads us home.

Rocks

Stone Mountain

Headed south on I-85 toward Atlanta,
a sense of surprise and wonder always confronts me.

There, rising above all else in the vicinity,
is Stone Mountain.

A granite mound that stretches for miles around,
far beyond that which is immediately visible.

And there, in the midst of hustle and bustle,
worries over being late for appointments,
anxiety over drivers not paying attention to the road,
and the ever-present possibility of fender-benders along the way,
she brings to me a momentary calm,
a sense that the God who pushed the mountains
from beneath the earth,
who made the rains to fall,
and the seas to rise,
the one who made grass to grow,
and trees to stretch above our heads—
that God is the one who watches over me
(and all the other drivers headed south on I-85.)

All Things Human

Here we are,
Human beings in the midst
Of all things human.

In our cars,
We rush when traffic rushes,
Sometimes we only crawl.

We pay attention,
To cars around us, billboards,
The sprawl of businesses,

All things human,
We adamantly declare, the rock,
Rising in the distance.

She, Stone Mountain,
Is there to argue against
Our human-centric thinking.

She is there—
Bold, firm, strong—declaring it's
Not all things human.

It's about God,
Rising above and in the
Midst of us all.

Chimney Rock

A rock,
Prominent in my childhood,
Breathtaking waterfall in the distance,
Vistas of the Blue Ridge
Spanning three hundred sixty degrees.

I yearn
To return, to recall the
Solidity of rock,
Beneath my feet,
To contemplate the shape
To which she owes her name.

A chimney,
Sometimes standing alone in a pasture,
The house, having long ago met her demise,
Sparks for us the notion of physical warmth but also the warmth
Of love shared among those gathered 'round the fireplace.

Chimney Rock,
Indeed, I long to return to you,
Your composition reminding me of the Rock
On which I stand, your chimney-shape
Recalling the fire, the warmth of God's love.

Sliding Rock

It's not Six Flags, nor Disney,
Feature rides engineered
By some of the best.

Instead, tucked away in Pisgah National Forest,
We find a water slide engineered
By God at creation.

The sixty-foot sloping boulder
Has as its fuel some 11,000 gallons of water
Per minute flowing across it.

And like Six Flags or Disney,
The promise of a thrill
Calls to children, youth, and even adults.

Filled with anticipation, they
Climb to the top, wait in long lines
'til time to take the plunge.

While they wait, adults make
Risk assessments, and parents lecture
Their young ones about points of danger.

But young ones, unable to listen, simply anticipate
Their adventure—the speed of the water, the thrill
Of their descent into the eight-foot pool at the bottom.

As crowds gather around Jesus, and more and more
Folks experience his miracles, disciples are proud,
Happy to be counted among his inner circle.

They pledge him their allegiance,
A willingness to be with him always,
To follow him wherever he might go.

But, like a parent with eager youngsters,
Jesus reminds that it's not only adventure—
Instead, a cost for following, for being his disciples.

In his wisdom, he knows the dangers that lie ahead,
And so he says to them, "Unless you are willing
To take up your cross, you cannot be my disciples."

Table Rock

The Cherokee saw in her a place
Of spiritual retreat, and in her shape they saw
A table on which the giant mythical chieftain
Took his meals, the shorter mountain being his footstool.

Ascending the rock, going to the mountain—
Important imagery for communing with God—
Sitting down at the table, reminiscent of the host
Who prepares the banquet and sets it before us.

Let me go there, go there again,
Not simply to idly walk the trails
Nor even to take in the beauty,
But help me to give thanks . . .

To God, our Rock,
To God who sits with us at Table.

Jump Off Rock

This place, bathed in beauty,
Receives a name rooted in tragedy,
Its background a mythical story from the Cherokee.

A message comes to the young maid
That her true love has been killed in battle,
Overcome by grief, she goes to the rock and jumps.

I wonder that she never experienced
A name change—something more pleasant—
This rock, this mountain called Jump Off Rock.

The calling of Christ in their lives, for early followers,
A jumping-off point for faith, but their experience with him—
How could they call it anything other than tragedy?

They waited behind locked doors, fearing for their lives,
But then came Sunday, and they renamed the tragedy,
They called it resurrection!

What's in a Name?

Name, name, what's in a name?
An adequate descriptor of what we all see?
An assignment despite the fact
We often don't agree?

She stood there, a giant granite monolith,
Yet some overlooked her completely,
Given the perch she provided for overseeing
The immense expanse of wonder and beauty.

Still, she deserved a name,
And so they looked at her
And tried to provide
Something fitting.

Some saw a head, thought of
A noble ruler centuries ago,
Others recalled stories of man's best friend
A Caesar who plunged to his death from her height.

Still others speak of a Cherokee word
That lost something in translation,
Do we ask again,
"Name, name, what's in a name?"

O Caesar's Head, however you came by your name,
On a couple of things we all can agree,
One, of your resplendency, and two, of your
Providing prominence overseeing inestimable beauty.

And when we plant our feet there
On your prominence, and the wind is blowing,
We can almost hear it whisper,
"Don't forget that God made it all!"

Brasstown Bald

She defies our imaginations
As to how she came to be,
Noble, rising nearly five thousand feet
Above the nearby town,
So tall as to create her own weather system—
Fog when it's clear down below,
Rain and sleet and snow
When there's nothing more
Than clouds in Blairsville.

All that having been said,
I'm clear that
Had Moses been in Georgia,
Called by God,
He would have tread
Through the dense fog,
Scaled the rock, the mountaintop,
To receive the twelve tablets, and that precipice
Would have been Brasstown.

Had Jesus been in Georgia,
Encountering John with
His message of repentance,
It would have been along the banks
Of the Chattahoochee, and there
The dance of who should baptize whom,
Then Jesus setting off on his
Hike through dense forest
To encounter Satan.

Satan would appear,
Would whisk Jesus away,
Set him atop a high pinnacle
Where he could see not only Georgia,
But North Carolina, South Carolina,
And Tennessee, and there he would promise
That God's holy angels would come
To his rescue should he take a leap
And cast himself off Brasstown.

And had Jesus been in Georgia,
When he proposed to Peter, James, and John
A retreat to the mountain to pray,
They would have made slow,
Calculated steps up Brasstown
Where they would have encountered
Great figures of faith—Moses, Elijah—
An experience so powerful that
They would offer to build booths and stay.

But Jesus would caution that while trips
To Brasstown are important for prayer,
For hearing words from God,
There is work to be done down below—
In Blairsville, Hiawassee, Hayesville,
Even to the far corners of the earth.

Adamant

Adamant—legendary rock
Said to be hard, impenetrable,
Just as we think of diamonds today.

Adamant—in our lives
To stand firm,
To refuse to change.

God's declaration over Israel,
Over us is that we
Are hard of heart.

Hard of heart, adamant,
Hearts set in wrong directions,
So how should we pray?

Convict us, O Lord, of our hardness of heart,
Open our hard hearts to the love of Christ.
Help us, instead, to be adamant in ways of peace and justice.

Rock, Paper, Scissors

It's a game we play—
Rock, paper, scissors.

Paper loses to scissors,
Scissors lose to rock,
But paper covers rock—for rock,
A loss.

But in real life the rock
Is a symbol for stability,
A foundation on which to build
Strong structures.

And so my prayer today—
Lord, make me a rock,
A firm foundation
In faith.

My Rock

Every child needs a rock,
Must have a rock
In order to survive,
And she was my rock.

Not too surprising should she
Fold under the weight,
Graduating, marrying, birthing two,
Then losing her true love.

A crushing machine turning boulders
Into mere pebbles could adequately
Describe her whirlwind life,
Yet, for me—for us . . .
She endured, she remained whole,
Not an easy task,
Grieving loss, finding support,
Doing all that was required,

In order that she be,
The rock for him
The rock for me,
So that we both . . .

Might be the people we
Are, my brother and
Me.

Mrs. Kennedy

Mrs. Kennedy—that was her name,
Suppose she had a first one,
But at the time never occurred to me
To ask.

Seemingly she was, in every way,
Average for a woman her age,
In those days—short, round, bedecked
In shirtwaists.

Oh, and I forgot to say,
Trips to the hairdresser,
Creating wafts of short curls with slight tints
Of blue.

But these days, my life review takes me
Back to her, back to where my journey began,
And I see things far from average
About her.

There was commitment, devotion, dedication
Evidenced by the fact that she
Showed up for decades to teach
Junior girls.

There was ease in her talking about the journey of faith,
And when she extended invitations to begin our own journeys,
Her warmth, her conviction urged me
To accept.

And so I walked the aisle, ripe age of nine,
It was my time and place to begin my journey, and I have
Never regretted it, but somehow I forgot to say thank you to
Mrs. Kennedy.

That's what we do in life—we forget to say thank you,
Forget to notice who was there at key moments in our lives,
But today, I reflect on my journey, and I say to Mrs. Kennedy,
"Thank you!"

His Rock

I was never privileged
to know him, his death long
before I came to know his son.

I listened to the stories,
emphasis one time in one place,
and another in a different telling.

About how they spent
every Saturday together,
just the two of them . . .

Straightening the house,
then uptown to the service station,
movie, picking up mom, dinner all three.

About how someone
would come by the house,
bending Jim's ear about hard times.

These would always set
Jim into motion, figuring out ways to help
even when his own bank account was low.

About times when someone around him
took the low road, maligning someone,
especially a person of color.

Jim would always take the high road,
standing up for the one unable
to stand up for himself.

I did my best to assign
a metaphor for the life of this one
who touched the life of my beloved.

I could not help but feel a sense of tragedy,
Jim's leaving this earth far too early
in my beloved's life.

But then I realized that in those short years
Jim gave him a lifetime of memories,
a book full of lessons.

And more than all that
Jim gave him the foundation
upon which to build a good life.

That's it!
I have the metaphor,
Jim was his rock.

Another Mrs. Kennedy

As did I, he had a Mrs. Kennedy,
Caretaker for him as a preschooler,
She dressed him in his tiny blue suit
And took him to his first funeral.

Maybe at that tender age he learned
To be comfortable with all matters of faith,
Even the ones that set the staunchest
Of adults on edge.

But besides that, she took him to Vacation Bible School
At her church, an added bonus
To V.B.S held at his own church
On an alternate schedule.

Then there were egg hunts on Easters,
Year after year, joy beyond measure
Since no such events occurred
In his own congregation.

Such simple things—such seemingly
Insignificant touches in a child's life,
But who can possibly measure the shaping
His Mrs. Kennedy gave to his life?

Calling Us

It was this place of our childhoods,
Always calling to us,
Calling our names,
Beckoning us to come.

It was a simple stream in our neighbor's pasture,
Simple but magical, made all the more so
By the vines swinging in the trees
And carrying us one side to the other.

But equally exciting was our table,
The mound of granite on which
We spread paper plates for our
Picnics of Vienna sausage with pork and beans.

Who knew these memories could anticipate our futures
Water, living streams calling us to begin
Lives of faith, and tables—granite and otherwise—
Spread with bread and wine, Christ's body and blood.

Tumbleweeds and Squishy Pillows

Sometimes we must admit
To being tumbleweeds
Blowing in the winds of faith,
Or perhaps squishy pillows
Conforming to whatever
Pressure comes from outside.

We may give passing nods
To desires to be Peter,
The Rock, upon which
Christ pledged to build the Church,
But truth be told, we're rather comfortable
Being tumbleweeds or squishy pillows.

And we rationalize any capacity
To grow or to change,
Saying that Peter, after all,
Was a Biblical person,
Not, in the least,
Like one of us.

But shall we, for the moment,
Confront our rationalizations?
Shall we remember the tumbleweed,
The squishy pillow that sometimes was Peter,
Shall we recall that instantaneous emergence
As Christ's Rock was never part of the story?

Shall we recall the sinking into the water,
The sleeping in the garden,
The "I do not know him" spoken three times,
And in so doing, may we put away all pretense
Of the vast expanse between ourselves
And the likes of Peter.

And may we give ourselves
Wholeheartedly to God,
Tumbleweeds, squishy pillows and all,
And may we say to Christ,
"Make of me a Rock upon which
To continue building your church."

A Place in the Rock

Sleep? Impossible
Because all I could do was worry.

How would things progress?
Slowly? Lightning speed?

Would I be strong enough,
And what would happen to ones left behind?

Turn off the worry?
I tried and failed.

Distract myself with other thoughts?
Only for brief moments in time.

Finally, exhaustion overtook the worries,
And I slept.

I awoke recalling the vivid details from the dream
And its accompanying calm, blissful feelings.

A mound rising in the distance
I recognize it—a huge rock.

And in the rock, a hollow spot
Big enough for my body, curled fetal position.

No need for dream interpretations,
Here I am—held—a place in the rock . . .

The Rock cradling me,
Whatever lies ahead.

Intrinsically Good, Intrinsically Bad

Intrinsically good? Intrinsically bad?
About most things
Hard to say.

Words, for instance,
Used to soothe a child,
Used to batter a neighbor.

Rocks? How about rocks?
Cold, hard instruments
As good a weapon as any other.

Rocks gripped in hatred,
Hurled at Stephen in an effort
To quell the story he sought to tell.

Words from Peter—sometimes braggadocious,
Three times in denial, yet Jesus' words made of this blustering one,
The rock upon which he would build his church.

Intrinsically good? Intrinsically bad?
About most things, it's all
In how we use them.

Stephen

They gathered in the church basement,
the faithful few teens,
their gathering time punctuated
with conversations about
what was going on in their lives.

On this night, they formed a litany:
"I failed my algebra test."
"Mrs. Smith is so mean."
"My parents are constantly on me about my grades."
"I overheard them talking about me behind my back."

A suitable time passed
And seemingly all complaints had settled into dust,
Only then did I suggest that we open our Bibles
And begin to read the chosen text,
Whereupon there was one more important complaint to voice.

"These Biblical people—they had it easy,
certainly no difficulties like all of us face!"
I let the complaint lie silent on the table
as we turned to Acts, chapter 7, and began to read,
"They rushed upon him and began to cast stones."

Smooth Stones

No tablets, no computers nor phones in hand,
At my house they find wonder and delight
In God's creation, exploring the backyard
And taking walks along the path into the woods.

A flower, a leaf, smooth stones,
They cram them all into their pockets,
And carry them in their hands, only to discover
That they can fill my deep pockets as well.

When home, they ask for paints,
And they begin their designs
On the smooth stones—flowers,
And ladybugs, their newest art motifs.

When time to go home, they bring me their gifts
Of smooth stones bedecked with flowers and ladybugs,
I cannot throw them away, and so I find places for them
In my garden and among my houseplants.

When they are gone and I am watering my plants,
These treasures remind me of joyous time together,
Somehow children know, and certainly God knows,
The power of simple things as reminders of love and care.

Otherwise why would God have the Israelites
To fish twelve smooth stones from the Jordon
And set them up, testament to God's love
And provision for yet another leg of their journey.

Cairn

They—young, inexperienced,
Yet confident of their own
Navigational skills—
Headed off into the woods.

They believed it simple
To follow the beaten path
That others before them
Had followed.

And if guidance proved
Necessary, most certainly
There would be the familiar
Orange or red or white blazes.

Deep in conversation
They barely paid attention
To their footsteps, but soon
Their path became less clear.

Only then did they realize
There had been no orange, nor red,
Nor white, and a bit of anxiety
Stirred within them.

Pledging resistance to fear,
They sat down to try and
Get their bearings, and there,
Near their chosen spot was a pile of rocks.

In due time, they headed off again,
Feeling only mildly confident
Of their chosen direction, but that's when
They noticed another pile of rocks.

The third siting of a pile of rocks
Convinced them that there may
Be something more intentional about
These piles of stone than originally discerned.

Only then did they notice
The specific number of stones
In each pile, but not only that,
The chosen resting spot for each stone.
Then and there they each gave silent thanks,
For simple stacks of stones,
For cairns given them
To show them the way.

And we say to God,
"Thank you for being our cairns."

Rock of My Salvation

Once,
When I was a child,
I stepped
Into a boggy spot
Near the water's edge.

Panic
Set in because my mind
Went immediately
To the T.V. cowboys
Neck-deep in quicksand.

Ankle-deep
Mud for me, I nonetheless
Called urgently
To my brother whose
Able hand rescued me.

Today
I am grateful for my Rock
Of Salvation,
And for others whose lives
Of faith have lifted me.

Roads

The Road up Saluda Grade

It wasn't as if
We were new to adventures:
Married—some would say too early—
Part-time jobs with college to finish,
A baby shortly thereafter—
Some would say too soon—
But then a move several states away
So he could go to seminary.

Tasks awaited us:
Packing, loading the rental truck,
Unloading the far-too-many belongings
Into the far-too-small apartment
Finding a job for the one,
Daycare for the little one,
Seminary matriculation for the other, but somehow
We focused all our anxieties one primary direction.

With deep consternation, we anticipated
A particular section of road,
Saluda Grade—narrow, steep, winding—
Room for disaster in many directions,
For an inexperienced rental truck driver,
As well as for the driver of the Pontiac that trailed behind,
And so Saluda Grade became the catch-all box
For every other worry.

If we could just survive her,
Then we could survive anything,
And so, the worry box tucked away for the moment,
The truck packed and ready to go,
He crawled into the too-high seat and with confidence
Put the truck into gear and began backing.
From my last task of sweeping the floor,
I ran out of the house shouting and waving my hands.

For, you see, from the front window,
I had just witnessed an unanticipated first worry come to pass.
Not Saluda Grade rising up in the distance, rather it was
The mobile home park's 55-gallon oil drum trash can,
Now crushed beneath the truck. So what could we do?
We could have chosen to open the worry box
And enclose a few more slips of paper into it,
But laughter was our medicine, our remedy for worry.
After surveying the flattened oil drum trash can,
He entered the truck once again and I the car,
And when we conquered Saluda Grade,
We gave thanks with an awareness that
God would always be with us on the journey,
That God would help us negotiate mountains—
Moves, job searches, and growing families—
And, in addition, would help us keep perspective,
And find laughter in such things as crushed trash cans!

Marvel and Give Thanks

Every time we witnessed
Someone else's misfortune—
The four-car pile-up,
The lone car spinning
Out of control,
Each of us said
Silent thank-yous
That it was not we
In that fix.

We made it through
The two-thousand-mile
Journey, save for the last twenty,
And that's when the doe,
Who, by the way, should have been
Bedded down by that
Time of night,
Decided to crash our car.

Home—we made it home,
But our car was far worse for wear,
Not only for the last twenty miles
But for many succeeding days,
We bemoaned our luck,
Car repairs that
Wouldn't be complete for
Two more months,
Worry about insurance premiums,

This, our third crash
With deer seeking only
To cross the road.

Advent—when we got home
It was just
Around the corner,
And immediately the story
Began to replay itself
In my head, interrupting
Thoughts about bad luck
And the litany of tasks
To be done.

A young couple
Heading out with
No GPS to guide the journey,
No comfortable LaCrosse
with lumbar supports,
No benefit from State Farm
Should something cause
A bump in the night.

And so, I put aside
Frustration and I confined
The to-do list to a spot
On the end table by the sofa,
And then I took time
To simply marvel
And to give thanks.

The Tail of the Dragon

They call it The Tail of the Dragon.

Promotional materials invite folks
Into the beauty of the Smoky Mountains.

Lush greens of spring and summer,
Red, orange, and yellows of fall,
Even the beauty of the deep forest
As the winter chill robs the trees of leaves.

And, of course, what they don't tell you
Is that some (me included) find it a terror,
These twists and turns, all 318 of them,
Along the simple 11 miles of road.

I'm sure I missed every thing of beauty
Glaring at me along the 11 miles,
For I was gripping my seat, and the doorframe,
Anything I could find.

Meanwhile others, some on motorcycles,
Seemed to be having the time of their lives,
Joyful banter even taking place
With other cyclists behind or in front of them.

Is this how I am, Lord,
Always gripping my seat,
Always afraid of what presents itself
Around the next twist in the road?

Draw my eyes up, Lord, and help me
See the beauty amid twists and turns along the road,
And make me confident that you will see me
Through it all.

Therapy

We start out in the morning
Without knowing where we are going.

If you haven't tried it,
You certainly should.

Along the mountainous roads,
I am able to forget myself. . .

And bills to be paid,
The beds to be made,
The week's worth of shopping,
The floors that need mopping,
The grass grown so tall,
My worries, one and all.

Thank you, O Lord, for this respite,
Shall we call this road, "Therapy?"

Fears

All of us have our fears,
Many of them irrational.

Elevators, spiders, needles—
But my personal one?

Fear of being hopelessly lost
While driving unfamiliar roads.

Once, when traveling to a new job
In Louisville, I missed my exit.

I found myself in Indiana,
And near-panic set in!

Maybe that's where
The fear originated.

But thank God that now
We have the GPS.

The little voice speaks to me,
Guides me along every twist and turn.

And thankful I am as well that God guides me
Along this path called life.

Big Red Apple 5-Mile Run

Little did they know,
Those kids of mine,
That most folks bought new shoes,
And trained for weeks to months.

After all, this stretch of road,
From the Big Red Apple at 1,486 feet,
Circled the tower on Chenocetah at
Some 1830 feet before it came back down.

But they? They simply tied on
Their well-worn sneakers,
And with nothing but confidence,
Began to run.

Lord, help us to throw off worries,
Give us faith, that though the course
Be sometimes tough, we run it
With carefree abandon!

US 221 to Little Switzerland

We made the trip.
It was
August 13, 1972.

Reveling in the joy of the day
For the two of us,
He guided the old Ford,
Bedecked inside with
Boxes of rice and
Outside with shoe polish
That never came off,
Along its route of US 221,
Our destination being
A quaint quasi-Swiss village
Tucked away in the heart
Of the Blue Ridge Mountains.

We made the trip.
It was
August 13, 2022.

Nostalgia present with us,
We loaded the car,
Our black Buick LaCrosse,
And found our way
Along some of the
Same sections of US 221
To the same

Quaint quasi-Swiss village
Tucked away in the heart
Of the Blue Ridge Mountains.

Thank you, O God,
For the beauty
Of a quasi-Swiss village
Tucked away in the heart
Of the Blue Ridge Mountains
And for the occasion that calls
Us there.

You Were There

You were there . . .

Old Caroleen Road,
College Drive,
Eighth Street,
Seminary Village Road,
Church Street,
Woodland Road,
Admiral Drive,
Innwood Road,
Summit Street,
Jones Road,
Morningside Drive,
Rock Springs Road,
Burwell Road.

You are here . . .

Jones Street.

The End of the Road

We often travel obscure roads,
The simple motivation of wondering
Where they will take us.

The paved road gives way
To gravel, the gravel gives way
To dust, ruts, and ridges.

Once, caught up in the delight,
Of dust, ruts, and ridges,
We came to an abrupt stop,

For the sign, totally unanticipated,
Said, "End of the Road,"
And I have since come to ponder . . .

Is this a metaphor for life,
All going well, wonder and delight,
When suddenly comes the end?

Wrap us in your arms, O Lord,
Keep us amid the wonder and the delight,
No worries about the end, for there . . .

Your arms embrace us.

Via Dolorosa

Other days you might have
walked this road easily,
hardly out of breath in reaching the top.

You were, after all,
strong, conditioned from tasks
in the carpenter's shop.

And you and the others
were accustomed
to walking wherever you went.

I can see you there
on the road, energetic, head held high
as you talked with them along the way.

How could they know
this road they'd taken easily
on other occasions would end like this?

Your back bent under the weight,
blood streaming from your back, your falling down,
then forced to get up and walk some more . . .

Your inability to carry the weight any longer,
the transferring of the load
to Simon of Cyrene . . .

The arrival at the prescribed destination,
appropriately called
The place of the skull . . .

How could they have imagined
this day-to-day road they traveled with you,
would one day be the *Via Dolorosa.*

Reflections

My Friend

My friend,
a woman of color, brushed
away tears as we sat
sipping coffee and reflecting
'round the table,
our feelings laid bare
about the latest police shooting
of a young black guy
in the street.

My friend,
when she'd gathered
her composure, said to us,
"You'll never know—
can't possibly know
unless you're black—
what it's like to
send your sons out
into the night.
And better be sure
to have those conversations,
about hands up,
no resistance,
else they won't
come home at all.

My friend—
what she said sure

made sense to me
and so I dared
quote her in a
sermon soon after
the news event.

My friend—
she must have
been right 'cause
boy, did it stir
emotions in that
white church of mine.
Seems white folks
don't like being confronted.
Racisim? Doesn't exist!
So my time in that church
was cut short!

My friend,
you taught me well!

A Nudge

Sometimes I think I can walk into a room
And find myself talking to the person
Carrying the biggest burden
Behind the brightest smile.

I stepped into the fellowship hall
For the reception given in my honor,
Me, the new pastor who'd only that morning
Preached her first sermon in the new church.

The wooden chairs spread themselves
Around the room, and without thinking
Much about where to choose to sit, I found
A spot close to Joe.

We exchanged pleasantries
The way you do when you're
Getting to know someone, but before long
Joe's smile dissolved from his face.

"It's been tough lately," he said,
"Just last year my twelve-year-old
Grandson accidentally shot himself in the last hour
Of the last day of deer season."

Those words forged the beginning of our relationship,
Not only that, but they also paved my entrance into
A church none too happy to receive
Their first woman pastor.

As women wiped tables and cleared desserts,
A few pulled me aside and said,
"We can't believe you sat down beside the person
In this room who needed you the most!"

I said nothing in response,
After all, what can you say to such a thing?
A sixth sense? Pure chance?
How about a nudge from heaven?

Quaking

We quaked in our boots
More than a little
That day for she
Spoke to our group—
New seminarians—about
Presuming to serve
The Great God of the Universe.

As the quaking subsided
A bit, we smiled to ourselves,
Realizing we were standing
In a long line of folks
Who'd said yes to the call.

And why were they able
To say yes to the daunting task?
Because they realized
The Great God of the Universe
Is also God With Us.

Carried, Crawling, Toddling

Seeing her first carried,
Then toddling, flanked
By her parents, was celebration
Enough each Sunday.

Made me think how
Inconsequential we are
As we meet the Great God of the Universe
There at the altar.

But God bids us come,
Carried, crawling, toddling,
However we may,
And as we approach we always hear . . .

"Well done, Child of Mine,
Now here,
Let me feed you!"

Carry Her

Some of us,
the older generation,
have our moments.

Sometimes jaded, we
overgeneralize, say things like
"What's to become of our world
with young things, unwilling
to get out of bed Sunday mornings
to bring their children to church?"

But there you are, corrections for
our careless chatter, and, chastised,
we watch as you carry her to the altar.

Gumbo

I rise
to make the gumbo,
cut the pods
into neat little segments,
then sauté them
ever so slightly,
just to the point
of negating the
undesirable slime.

I peruse the refrigerator
and locate the veggies
chopped last night—
onions, red pepper,
green pepper, and celery—
into my oil-bathed iron skillet
they go, my dutiful stirring
and breathing in
the savory sweetness,
then turning my hand
to the remaining tasks
of slicing the andouille
into bite-sized pieces,
readying the shrimp,
then pouring it all
into the broth
that will hours later
delight our palettes.

The chopping, the blending,
the sweet smells
pervading my kitchen
turn my thoughts
in another direction,
and I remember—
remember a morning
endeavor I should
never forget—
for I am blessed,
a warm home,
food awaiting
the cooking endeavor,
a husband soon to rise
at the behest of aromas
that beckon him.
And so I stop,
gumbo simmering
in the Dutch oven
on top of the stove,
and I make my way
to the side porch,
my special place
for rest and for prayers.

Father Robert

New to the South,
He hurries in ways
Foreign to natives.

Speech—that too,
Comes so fast they sometimes
Scratch their heads
Hoping the lost words
Are not keys to understanding
Their journeys toward heaven.

But look—see the difference—
The slow, deliberate way
He pauses with each one
At the altar—
The hurting,
The worried,
The afraid—
His gentle touch
On their foreheads,
The sign of the cross
Reminders for them of
The Great Healer.

Thanks be to God!
He knows when
To slow down.

There Was a Rumor

There was a rumor floating 'round,
The kind that ends with the words,
"It's true."

But you know how rumors go,
Something you know you tell me, something I know, I
Tell you.

And both of us tell the same way
Told to me, told to you, so then it surely, most certainly must
Be true.

So they were all happy in the church down the street,
Happy as any Methodists you ever
Could meet.

Happy with their pastor and his two-plus children,
Happy, though struggling, they hadn't yet closed
The door.

In a meeting in the church council they heard the
News straight from the Bishop, "Not necessary. Needn't take
The vote!"

And so they all shook their heads,
And in agreement, for now they would stay in
The denomination.

That is until the church in the very next town
Met and took their vote. That's when the
Rumor started . . .

The one she told me, and then I, of course,
Told you, meaning, of course, it's true, we all simply
Must vote!

God, You Must Have a Sense of Humor

Ministers maintain their lists,
store them in a file somewhere deep
inside their brains—their comparisons—
the good and bad, the better or worse
points between the old assignment and the new.

This was a conversation that took place
with myself alone, "At least," I said
in my one-sided discussion, "At least I won't
have to get up at the crack of dawn Thanksgiving morning
to go crack eggs alongside my peers
for folks looking for a reunion breakfast
with friends returning home, none of whom really
need another big meal that day,
only to go home to cook
a big meal for my own family.
For all the good in this place—that one I won't miss!"

Imagine my consternation,
about the get-to-know-you visit
with parishioners in the new church
where the conversation began like this:
"We're so proud of our church," says one member,
to which I said with a smile, "Oh, tell me more!"
"Well, we have this ministry to the homeless
who spend their nights at the Salvation Army up the street."
I nodded, already anticipating pride in my new church
showing concern for the homeless.

"Yes, we get here about five o'clock both on Easter
and Christmas mornings to begin cooking—
eggs, bacon, sausage, grits, biscuits—
the whole nine yards and serve them at their tables,
sit and talk with them—the best ministry we've ever done!"

It would take a while before God would convict me
of my self-absorbed-ness, before I would hear God
say, "If you're going to talk the talk, you better
walk the walk!"

Right then all I could say to God was,
"God, you must have a sense of humor!"

Pictures of God

Most of us, when asked about our families,
Are happy to whip out wallets,
And begin the recitation,
"This is my oldest, along with his oldest . . ."
Flipping the plastic sleeves until the other
Grows weary.

Most of us, when asked about God,
Have fuzzier pictures,
But pictures nonetheless,
I confess in some of my pictures
God is scowling,
Wagging a finger, telling us to set
Things right.

Ah, to claim more beautiful pictures,
More beautiful pictures
Of God.

I remember a time,
The week before his fiftieth,
He stayed with her in the hospital,
Began to see the seriousness of her situation,
While I began to sneak around, and plan
His celebration,

Just before he was to arrive home,
Guests to surprise him in the back yard,

He called to say, "It's cancer, she hasn't much time
To live."

So what do you do?
Send guests home?
Quickly change out of Hawaiian attire?
Begin the process
Of grieving?

The voice whispered, "No, go on with plans,
Enjoy the food, sing as the guitar and banjo play.
That's when I saw the picture,
God in a Hawaiian shirt,
Moving to the music,
And raising a glass,
"Happy birthday to you,
My child."

Pictures

With her young pupils
She had the habit of asking them
    To draw her a picture
    Of first one thing and then another.

After all, for young ones,
lacking writing skills, pictures bear the weight
    Of their stories,
    Happy or sad or anywhere in between.

I looked silently into the eyes of the congregation
My heart begging them to paint me a picture . . .
    A picture of what God is doing in their lives,
    And one by one they obliged.

There was the picture of the young adult
Newly-attached to her significant other
    Whose picture was of a gift, the young man
    With whom she chose to spend her life.

There was that of a young mother
Who, as she gently swayed,
    Crafted an image of thanksgiving
    Which, of course, included the little one she held in her arms.

There was that of a father,
His picture surrounded by darkness
    From the near-tragedy recently come to his family,
    But here and there bright colors conveyed glimmers of hope.

There was that of another,
Tears erupting from all sides,
     Yet we are to understand they are tears
     Of vastly different types . . .

Tears of sadness from being misunderstood,
Rejected, dismissed as if hardly a person at all,
     But tears of joy from being loved, accepted,
     Drawn into a family of faith who loves him just as he is.

In a Row

We watched,
Traffic completely halted,
Because Mother Duck chose
That precise moment
To parade her
Little ones from
Lakeshore one side
Of the road to
Lakeshore the other side.

Amazing! She lined
Them up behind her
With a few
Simple quacks and they
Made their journey.

You and I—we wait
Impatiently for our ducks
To line up in a row.

Then, we tell ourselves,
Then, we will be happy,
Then, we will be grateful,
Then, we will proclaim
That life is good—
A gift.

Like a mother duck
God calls us
On a journey,
And more than that
God calls us to
Find joy,
And gratitude,
And to proclaim
That life is good . . .

Even when our ducks
Don't line up
In a row.

Found

In our early almost-wakefulness,
You call our names,
In the blazing noonday sun,
You call our names,
In the cool breezes of an afternoon garden,
You call our names,
In the quiet of evening,
You call our names.

Oh Lord,
Would that we
Could all be,
Like tiny Oscar,
As I play a game
Of hide-and-seek
With him, and as I
Playfully call to him.
"Oscar, where are you?"
Whereupon he responds,
"Here I am!"

In the midst
Of life, O Lord,
In the midst of wrongdoings
That we contrive
May we desire,
Nothing more from You,
Than to be
Found!

Swan Song

Awoke
to the realization
of time
marching rapidly on,
long past the diagnosis.

Unnerved,
near panic becomes
my reality,
accomplishments expected in
remaining time given me.

Prayer—
Could it be
the answer
to the riddle,
what's expected of me?

Expectations?
Feed the hungry?
Find solutions
to world poverty?
Some grand swan song?

Silence,
my closest companion,
Not answers,
Just continued questions,
I pursued daily tasks.

Music,
the church choir,
and words
blasting my consciousness
'til confined to paper.

This?
My swan song?
Your answer
to the riddle,
Make music, write poetry?

Marching into Heaven

I want to think
That in my march
All will be bliss.

All bitterness, all resentment,
All anger gone, my having heard
The call heavenward.

But certain things
I clutch fervently
Even to the core of my being.

Like the time
The good church lady
Could hardly wait 'til the service was over . . .

Whereupon she began her attack,
Castigating me for my prayer,
With my thinking, "A prayer of all things!"

"Hate crime?" she said,
Wagging a finger, "All my news sources
Say not a hate crime at all!"

My blood boiled within me,
And my voice raised to levels
Perhaps inappropriate to church.

"You're going to tell me
That shooting eight Asians point-blank
In the face isn't a hate crime?"

Of course, she stormed out of church
Taking her husband
And church membership along with her.

So those kinds of things
Still disturb my quietude
Even far along the journey.

And I am left to ask
"God, is it possible to march into heaven
Still angry—angry about injustice?"

Let It Go

I had a dream,
One so real
As night becoming day.

In the dream
God called to me,
Told me to begin my march.

I knew it
To be a long journey
So I left swiftly.

But I remembered
To grab a solitary thing,
A life-long project.

The sheaf of papers
Taped neatly together,
My collected questions.

Questions about the world,
Things that had wrenched me
To the core of my being.

Before many steps
On my long journey,
I saw the first sheet . . .

The tape mysteriously dissolving
The page, then, wafting
Quietly away on the wind.

A second of earthly
Time passed in which I felt panic—
The type common to us on earth.

In the panic
I clutched the remaining sheets
All the more determinedly.

I began, though, to focus
On the journey,
Sites and sounds along the way . . .

Beauty such as I
Could never have imagined
Invaded my senses.

All thewhile
Page after page began to unravel
And disappear into the wind.

As continuous beauty
Invaded my senses I suddenly noticed that
I clutched but a single sheet in my hand.

Once again I felt a moment of panic,
For I knew the last page to contain
The most pressing question of all . . .

Injustice—to me—to others—
"Why, God? Why?"
But suddenly there was a whisper . . .

A whisper that boomed loudly
As it fell on earth and echoed throughout heaven,
And this is what the whisper said . . .

"Let it go!"

How Can I?

How can I cry out to you,
O God? For I sit in
My warm home, safe and secure,
While lives of
Brothers and sisters
Get ripped asunder?

Do I presume too much?
Do I have even a hint
Of their pain
When all I see
Are split-second images
Spread across the T.V?

Still, O God,
Can we leave
Them to cry alone,
To scream the injustice
And to plead with you
To intervene?

And if you
Have not yet
Heard their cries,
Shall we, our whole world,
Join in, sheer numbers
Causing rumbles in heaven?

And then, O Lord,
Will you hear our cries,
Will you be moved to act
Bringing an end
To evil that seems
For the moment to win?

Linkletter

Linkletter had it right,
"Kids say the darndest things,"
But sometimes it's not the kids say
The darndest things.

They watched me that day,
Watched me walk the aisle
To begin my journey, and later I
Overheard their words.

"Hope she's doing it for
Right reasons, not just because
A friend walked the aisle
Just last week!" they said,

As if the journey need be about
Blinding lights or dramatic turns
From decades-long lives
Filled with sin.

No! No decades for me
This point in time, I only knew
I wanted this faith Mrs. Kennedy
Described so simply.

Linkletter, you're right,
But only so far, for sometimes it's not the kids
Say the darndest things, sometimes
It's the adults.

To Share

He,
Always more generous
Than I . . .

He
Stuffs five-dollar bills
Driver's-side compartment.

He
Hands to those
Bearing signs.

I,
The cynical one,
Ask questions.

I
Wonder, "They really
In need?"

I
Say, "Maybe only
A scam!"

I
Interject, "Possibly support
Their habit."

Then,
Generous Soul, says,
"Doesn't matter!"

"We—
We're simply called
To share!"

Dangling by a Thread, Hanging in the Air

I passed by quickly—no surprise in that,
For I'm always hurrying somewhere,
This time simply passing by, dining room window,
When I spotted her . . .

Dangling by a thread, hanging in the air,

But, of course, it required a second look
A re-tracing of my steps,
Before I could be sure—she a last vestige of maple's color
Suspended, a seeming magic trick.

Instead, dangling by a thread, hanging in the air.

She became our wonder, our delight,
Her size, her weight, the stirring breezes,
Surely all of those would prove
Too much and spell her demise, she . . .

Dangling by a thread, hanging in the air.

We watched days on end, and silently,
We each placed our wagers,
How long would she last, would we see
Her all this day, and even into tomorrow . . .

Dangling by a thread, hanging in the air?

Made me think of life, how easily we
Become that one—dangling in seeming jeopardy,
But please, those of you who see me,
Never, place grim odds on me.

For I am held,
Held by a single invisible thread.

Spoiled Brat

She never stops to realize how much they've done already,
Doing without themselves so she could have new clothes,
Scrimping and saving for her college education.

Yet, in her desires, she is insatiable,
She asks, and asks, and asks for more,
Shall we call her a spoiled brat?

Here I am, living my seven decades,
Perfect health until of late,
Wonderful parents, husband,
Children and grandchildren,
Warm home, plenty of food to eat,
Yet, all I can do
Is to beg for more,
A miracle of healing,
More years upon this earth,
More time with them,
The people I love.

So what shall you call me,
O God, my Creator,
Will you call me your spoiled brat?

Lifesaver

Like a hard, unyielding
Lump, stuck in my throat,
Impossible to get it up,
Futile trying to swallow it,
There you are,
Stuck.

I am stuck,
Can't move on,
Can't find my old self,
Can only feel the pain,
Day after day, with you, hard lump, I am
Stuck.

Then I remember the Lifesaver,
Hard, still threatening should it
Slide unbidden, stuck
In my throat, but, while hollow, it
Allows me to
Breathe.

Lord, you know me,
Know my every struggling
Moment, so here,
As I struggle even to
Breathe, be my
Lifesaver.

Blue-Haired Ladies Have Places On the Pews

Blue-haired ladies have places on the pews,
If any doubt, ask my mom who, in the fifties,
Lived the mortification of her four-year-old,
Unable to whisper, asking why the lady
In front of them had blue hair!

Normally Mom would have been full of pride,
Her four-year-old sitting with her in church
But on this day, she gladly would have given
Up her place on the pew, glad if only the floor
Would swallow her up, along with her embarrassment.

But four-year-old little boys,
Like the little ones who came to Jesus, need never be hindered,
Not even with their troublesome questions about rinses
That promise to blot out the gray while at the same time casting
An undeniable blue hue to coiffures such as that of Mrs. Smith.

But more than places on the pews,
Blue-haired ladies,
Embarrassed mothers,
And especially curious little boys,
All have places at the altar.

They'll Know We Are Christians

They created a litany,
The story of their church. Loving? Caring?
They thought themselves the epitome.

With a very-near swagger,
They boasted about their youth,
Told of them, chapter after chapter.

Sent them off each Sunday to the basement choir room,
And there they rehearsed the music that for all
Would be a spirit's boom.

The sixties, times were troubling for them,
And word reached the church that
Folks were coming, trying to get in.

 Problem was, these folks had dark skin,
So lock the door, let them knock,
But don't let them in.

Still singing, voices floating like doves,
As they stood, locked outside,
"They'll Know We are Christians by Our Love."

Scraps

She never discards a single one,
A piece of this, a scrap of that,
Solids, stripes, and flowers—
Tucked here, stored there.

At the moment she cannot imagine
The whole that they will create, but in time,
She will sew them together,
Log cabin, flying geese, or wedding ring.

I am standing here, Lord,
Standing and looking at the scraps
That are my life,
So take them, sew them together . . .

Make the pattern that is pleasing,
In your sight.

O Rest in the Lord

I tire easily and overwhelmingly,
A deep and abiding fatigue
That begins and ends in my bones.
With the Psalmist I cry out,
"How long, O God, how long?"
And the words that come back
Are convicting ones—about striving
For achievement and relentless effort—
An unending human race.

But now, O God, even as
I face the error of my own ways,
Let me rest!
Let my tired bones, heart,
And soul rest in you!

Ah, the Saints!

Ah, the Saints!
> Peter, Thomas, Matthias,
> And all the rest!

Their hands
> Folded in prayer,
> Held children on their laps,
> Brought the sick and the lame
> Into the presence of Jesus.

Ah, the Saints!
> Those in our day
> Whose hands fold in prayer
> Who care for children,
> Who attend the needs of the hurting,
> Who make a place at the Table
> For those otherwise excluded!

For all the saints—may God bless you and give you peace!

Believe

In the beginning God created
the heavens and the earth . . .
and God saw that it was good.

You ask me to believe, O God,
that you were there from the beginning,
that you called the earth, the sea, and the sky,
into existence, and to believe that it all is for good.

The Lord said to Abram, "Go from your country,
your people, and your father's household
to the land I will show you . . . and I will
make you a great nation."

You ask me to believe, O God,
that you have a calling, a claim
upon each of our lives, that as we honor
your calling good things come to pass.

Blessed are the poor,
for yours is the kingdom of heaven,
Blessed are you who hunger now,
for you will be satisfied.

You ask me, O God, to believe
that though trials, difficulties
exist in this life, you reverse
them all for good.

For God so loved the world
that he gave his only Son
that whosoever believes in him
should not perish but have eternal life.

You ask me to believe—
believe in the redeeming power
of the love of Christ,
in the wisdom of resting my life in his.

In my Father's house are many rooms;
and if I go to prepare a place for you,
I will come again, and will take you to myself
that where I am you may be also.

You ask me to believe in something
beyond this life, beyond this world,
to trust that there is a forever
in your presence.

It's a lot to ask, O God,
a hard task to discover seeds of faith,
to plant them in my life, and so I say,
I believe, O God. Help my unbelief.

Fishermen, Fishermen

Fishermen, fishermen,
Your fathers were fishermen,
And likely their fathers before them,
But we can't know for sure.

They taught you to love the sea,
The feel of nets between your fingers,
The joy of the catch
On a good day.

But from them you also learned
Patience for times of waiting
Just like the farmer for the harvest,
And persistence when the catch doesn't come.

Any wonder that Jesus called to fishermen?
Must've been hard to hear him ask
You to put down your nets and follow,
But then, of course, he spoke your language . . .

"I will make you fishers of men!"

Ellenboro

Ellenboro—
the place of my birth
but barely a wide place
in the road.

Forest City—
itself a small town, but often,
for recognition's sake, I
claim it as my birthplace instead.

Nazareth—
your hometown,
not Jerusalem as everyone expected,
and so they questioned your origins.

Questions—always questions—disturbed they asked,
"Can any good come out of Nazareth?"
the inquiry stemming from an assumption that good things
come only from big places, notable places on earth.

Nazareth—
we're here to say that good came out of you,
that good came out of His life,
His ministry, his death.

Ellenboro—
I claim you. May we claim all our wide places in the road,
And may good come from them as we witness
To the love of Christ in all our Ellenboros.

Thoughts While Gardening

My mind wanders
A million different directions
When I'm in my garden,
No doubt the same
As for gardeners through the generations.

This time I'm bemoaning
The weed-pulling task
That faces me as I prepare
For squash, beans, and cucumbers.

Those gardeners those millenia ago—
Did they wipe sweat from their brows,
And curse the weed-pulling task?
Maybe that's why they began asking questions—
About how it all began and why life seems so hard.

And there came the story—
One about a beautiful garden
Where things are blissful
Where not a single weed is allowed to grow—
Not until there was temptation,
Until the one gave in, tempted her mate as well.

"You might know it!" they thought,
"It just had to be a woman!"
And the story has been told
In a million, billion variations ever since,
And when I'm gardening, I shout, "Enough!"

Sometimes

Sometimes
I just want to
Escape, to say,
I've done my do.

Time to check out,
Sit back and rest
On my laurels, even move on
To a better place.

After all, been on this old earth
More than seventy years,
Worked hard, believed,
Tried to make a difference.

But this world's problems
Are beyond me,
Don't know what to do,
Where to begin.

Much easier just to check out,
To say, "Turning this show over
To a new generation, let them
Solve problems my generation helped create."

"What's that, Lord?"
What's that, you say?
Not my time—my time to go?
And, therefore, not time to check out?"

"What? What is it you go on to say,
That as long as here on earth
Still time to work,
To join hands, young and old . . .

To make the world a better place."

Musings of a Wife-Mother-Minister

"I'm here!"
"I'm here," I say,
panting, out-of breath,
waiting as if to be checked
off in the black book of
my grade school teacher
as she calls our names,
then looks up in disbelief
as someone rushes in
long past the bell
and calls, "Present!"

My body still tense,
I wait to see what it is
that you need.

It takes time,
but finally,
finally I realize—

you need nothing
from me.
You don't need . . .

me to find your glasses
or to cook your breakfast
or to balance the checkbook.

or to listen to a problem
or to take care of the grandchildren
or to work on the family calendar.

or to explain why children ran in the sanctuary last Sunday
or why giving is down this month
or why the toilet is stopped up when it is brand new!

You don't need me!
When I say, "Present,"
the work is done . . .

at least on my part.
I suspect
yours is only begun!

Me-ness

Please hear me, O God,
I need to confess.

For you have reached out,
Convicted me the deep error
Of my ways.

It is not my meanness, O God,
Offenses against my brothers and sisters,
Rather it is my me-ness that makes me,
Unable to see brothers and sisters in need.

This Good Day

I was born for this day,
This good day.

I was born to rise,
To call my husband from bed.

I was born to brew coffee,
And to share a cup with him.

I was born to ride passenger's seat
As we make our way to church.

I was born to write poetry,
To share it with others who grieve.

I was born to make music,
To blend piano and voice in praise of God.

I was born for this day,
This good day.

My No, Your Yes

What violence might
They do to me, I would have questioned,
And if not outright violence
What shunning might take place,
To me, to a mom and dad
Who certainly don't deserve it?

And what about him,
Insults about me,
The kind of woman
I must be, how he
Need only say the word
And they'd put an end to me!

If issued an invitation to mother your Son,
O God, I'm sure I'd have said a sounding, "No!"
But you, O Blessed One? You are a testament
To trust and faith, and I'm glad
You said yes!

The Star

You know the drill,
Wrap in tissue paper,
Place carefully in the box,
Store in the attic
'til another year.

But when another year
Rolls around and you
Pull the things from
Their attic storage,
Inevitably Mary has
A chip in her robe,
Or Joseph's staff has broken,
Or the star has fallen
From the pottery tree
Made by little hands.

Quickly, glue gun in hand,
We do the work of
Resurrecting stars and
Fixing blemished nativities.

So glad we weren't
In charge of things
Like announcements
To Mary and Joseph
Or travel to Bethlehem
Or hanging a star
Over a stable.

A Stable and Straw

I remember well
How happy he was,
He, the soon-to-be dad
For the first time.

And though he had
Always cherished me,
In those days, he wanted
To give me sun, moon, and stars.

And what about him,
Loving her, cherishing her,
Trusting God despite
Jeers and sneers from others?

He must have wanted
To give her sun, moon, and stars,
But, instead, there was only a bright star
Shining in the sky . . .

A stable and straw for a bed.

How Lucky!

How lucky you were,
The decision virtually
Taken off your plate!

My husband and I
With our first?
Well, we deliberated . . .

And deliberated,
And deliberated,
And finally made our decision.

We even phoned relatives
The moment he was born,
And told them his name.

It was time to leave the hospital
And the nurse came in demanding
A name for the birth certificate.

And he vowed that most certainly
Our little one didn't look like
A David at all!

Can you see the trouble you escaped,
The decision handed you,
After all, by an angel?

But here's the question that
Pops into my head,
"Were there moments . . ."

"Were there moments
You looked at him and thought,
'Doesn't look like *Yeshua!*'"

Did that thought continue with you
Through many days, perhaps even
'til you knelt at the cross?

At the Manger

I arrived at the manger
Ready to fall on my knees,
To raise my arms
And fold my hands in prayer.

But suddenly a force
Beyond my comprehension
Whisked me away and carried me
Lightning-speed as if above a movie set.

We—the force and I—paused
In mid-air suspension
At points I discovered were scenes
Scattered through my life.

Scene one—the grocery story
Where I waited, grumbling, behind
An old woman rifling through coupons and digging
Through her change purse for the last necessary coin.

Then the scene beyond the scene—
The old woman receiving her meager
Social security check and wondering
How to make it last 'til month's end.

I conjured energy to resist
The incomprehensible force but it whisked
Me away 'mid screams of "I'm sorry,
I didn't know."

The next scene a patch of tall grass
By the interstate ramp
A man standing there with a sign,
"Will work for food."

We pause there long enough
To hear me whisper under my breath,
"Right! Work—maybe!
Then take the proceeds to buy yourself a drink!"

Then the scene beyond the scene—
The man, stripped and broken,
Lost job, lost family, lost home
After military service and PTSD.

No resolve imaginable could
Stop the momentary pauses along my life's path
Where each time I found myself repeating
The refrain, "I'm sorry. I didn't know."

Finally, all movement stopped,
The force suddenly whisked me up and deposited me
Back where I had begun, but I was too broken,
Too sorrowful to lift my arms in prayer.

And so, the force lifted them for me,
And it whispered in my ear.
"Now you are ready,
So call out to God as you kneel at the manger."

Best Things Ever

It's one of the best things ever—
Showing off a newborn,
Showing off a two-year-old.

You must have been beaming,
Shepherds showing up
From the fields nearby.

And even more joyful, the visit of
Wise Men from the East.
Is this some sort of indication . . .

An indication of ways he
Will be received, honored, worshipped
Throughout his entire life?

Time will tell,
But for now,
It's the best thing ever!

Smudges

She showed up and hoisted
Her barrage of items haphazardly onto the
Conveyer in her local grocery.

The next customer, puzzled, pointed
Toward her forehead asking the pressing question,
"The meaning—your letter X?"

Across town—along the grimy
Assembly line—one spots something amiss—this
Also, center of his co-worker's forehead.

Something clearly different here from
The usual grim and dirt, so he offered
His gift—a clean, white handkerchief.

Thank you, God, in your wisdom
You allow crosses turned askew or unusual
Smudges in a dirty worksite as opportunities—

Opportunities to boldly proclaim faith—
Our belief that "Dust we are, and
To dust, we shall return."

Alleluias

Joyfully we sang our alleluias,
With Lent in view, these
To be our last for a time.

The little one
Came to church with scant
Awareness of hymns
Or prayers or much of what
We do in church, but somehow
She clung to the word.

The last chord sounded,
There was a brief pause,
And then, as if to honor
Father, Son, and Holy Spirit,
She spoke aloud her solo,
"Alleluia, alleluia, alleluia!"

And God looked down
Upon the earth and said,
"It is good!"

Icon

Dreamed a dream.

An icon appeared,
The strokes of paint
Etched his silhouette,
Then captured his features.

I studied sunken
Cheekbones, and sad
Eyes, pictures of
Suffering and fatigue.

But then the
Dream morphed, and
I saw his arms,
Big and sinewy.

Those arms—they were
Reminders of a God-given strength,
A gift that extended
All the way to the cross.

The icon, then, etched itself
Deeply into my brain,
And any time my strength
Begins to fail, I conjure its memory.

Mary Magdalene and Others

She was there alone—
alone to do her work—
women's work,
the lone, difficult work of grief.

It's not as if the others aren't sad
But they have work to do too,
Making sense of the story
Gone completely awry.

There alone, she realizes
She must hurry home,
Home to report that
The stone has been rolled away.

The others all stand,
Listen to the horrific report,
Then Peter and John spring into action,
Making a foot race to the grave to conduct . . .

A thorough investigation and, if possible,
To set aright the supposed robbing of the grave,
The added insult to the injury
They'd already endured.

Still alone in her grief work
There came a disruption,
And Mary felt a presence with her,
One she assumes to be the gardener.

"*Please*," she says to him,
"*Please tell me where you've laid him.*"
A few more interchanges and the Risen Christ
Speaks her name!

Her work takes a radical turn,
Her work becomes that of announcing
That the One Crucified
Is now the Christ Risen!

It is not her work alone,
For God calls us to join her,
To announce the good news
Of a Christ who conquers death.

Beyond Comprehension

It's beyond comprehension—

Her kneeling there
at the feet of her eldest,
watching his labored breathing,
taking in the signs
that the end was near.

There must have been
those who urged her,
"Just go back home,
You needn't be here,
to the bitter end—too painful."

She must have smiled,
grateful for their concern,
Her response?"
"I'm fine. I'll stay.
Where else would I be?"

No doubt the day grew long,
tears filling her eyes many times,
as she experienced joyful flashbacks
of their lives together while also
filled with regret for good times cut short.

It's beyond comprehension . . .

The tired footsteps
that led from the borrowed tomb,
she, all the while,
trying to make sense of it
and find one shining glimmer of hope.

Upon Him

Woke up this morning
Feeling a general sadness,
Not so much my own
But the sadness of the world.

Feels heavy, feels like too much
For any shoulders to bear,
But then I remember,
Remember the cross,
The weight of it upon
His shoulders, carried
Not for himself but
For all of us.

And I remember
He calls us
To cast our burdens
Upon him.

Consider the Lilies

"Consider the lilies," you say?
Maybe I'll consider this one,
One cast aside after
Making its debut on Easter.

That day, despite your reputation for glory
Exceeding that even of Solomon,
Either someone takes you home or you wind up
In the trash along with the morning's coffee cups.

So, I chose you, though I know not why,
After all, claiming no green thumb
I had few expectations as I dug the hole
And placed you into the red Georgia clay.

Summertime drought with no watering
From my hand, you crinkle then fade
Into winter's oblivion, but in spring
Your resilience begins to show.

Stored energy and strength make
Leaves to form, and then, late May,
Even early June you break forth into bloom
And once again challenge Solomon in all his glory!

And now, O God, as I consider this lily,
Free me from worry, bathe me in faith
In you who watches over lilies
And cares for the likes of me.

A Flower on the Lord's Cross

Easter morning—
the first I would experience
while serving this church.

I was witness
To the giant cross
Posted securely on the sidewalk.

I learned that
the one in charge of the cross-decorating event
was an aging florist who secured box upon box
of damaged but still luxurious flowers.

Ms. Braid, the soft-spoken but commanding woman
with decades of experience with flowers extended the invitations
to church members showing up to cook the meal.
I can see her to this day, pushing flowers into our hands,
and smiling as the cross began to take shape.

I did the pastoral thing of greeting members
who showed up to make the meal, wishing each a Happy Easter,
and I made it a point to also be on hand as each van-load
of scruffy, homeless persons arrived
from their night's lodging at the Salvation Army.

I can hear her voice to this day,
her soft r's from her coastal upbringing
still ringing out her invitations

to first one scruffy, big and burly,
homeless man and then another.

"Don't ya want to put a *flowuh* on the *Lahrd's* cross?" she said.
True confession—I cringed a bit, "Why would any big, burly
homeless man want to put a *'flowuh* on the *Lahrd's* cross?'"
when he can already smell Southern breakfast smells
coming from the kitchen just off the sidewalk?"

I never gave it much thought at the time,
but I did notice that not a single big, burly
homeless man rejected Ms. Braid's invitation
to "put a *flowuh* on the *Lahrd's* cross,"
despite the smells of bacon, and eggs and biscuits.

Maybe it's the slowing down of life,
the wisdom of aging,
or that the most important lessons in life
simply take time, but whatever the reason,
I get it! I understand!

Not a single big, burly homeless man groused
nor resisted Ms. Braid's invitation,
hurrying on by for his best breakfast in weeks.
Instead, each took the *flowuh* in hand
and placed it methodically on the cross.

Why? Because in the invitation
Each felt included!
After all, flowers and especially crosses are not
just for the polished, just for those sitting on pews in church,
But for everyone!

One and Done

All too often
That's what they are,
One-and-done,

Taking their places,
Along the altar,
Arranged and fussed over,

These, the forced blooms,
Charm our sensibilities
For the one day of days.

But after that?
All too often
Cast aside, forgotten.

The authorities hoped
That's what would
Happen to him . . .

Hung on a tree,
Cast aside into
A borrowed tomb.

Who would remember
Someone who'd faced
Such a humiliating death?

Some of us
Take them home. Me?
I give them their own bed.

Today I water them
And I wait, wait
For fragrant white blossoms.

Late May—even June?
Nature designed them
That way.

Not the forced
Blooms of the greenhouse, and he?
Nothing forced about his mission.
I'm happy, happy to have them
Resurrected in my garden,
Reminders of him.

Deepest Purpose

Give me a
New job to do,
A new sense of purpose,
That or a sign,
Confirmation in the
Work I am already doing.

After all,
Time is ever so short,
And I need to know
That I have
Fulfilled my deepest purpose
When I leave . . .

This world.

One Life

If I have but one life—
and I do—
I want it to be lived in trust and faith,
trust and faith in you.

If I have but one life—
and I do—
I want the years and the days,
Even the minutes and seconds to count . . .

Count for you, and I want the fact
That I walked this earth
To have mattered,
Mattered for you.

So, help me, O God,
Help me chart my path,
This one and only life,
A sweet gift from you.

To the Bitter End

I can't tell . . .

Do I really hear your voice,
Or is it my imagination
playing tricks on me?

Those on the outside
Always criticize us,
Laugh and say it's all a great big hoax.

I've never had
so much trouble before,
But isn't that always true?

Times are good,
We bow and say "Thank you"
but altogether different as times are bad.

And when it's a very,
Bad—those times especially
We wonder, "Are they true . . .

These stories of faith and can I
Really hear your voice
Whispering reassurance, saying you'll be with me?"

For now I choose to believe,
Choose to trust the words
Hanging in the wind rustling in my ear . . .

"I'll be with you to the bitter end."

Maze of Faith

I followed them,
For they said it would be fun,
Finding our way
Through the dense shocks of corn.

I was intrigued,
Hearing their laughter,
Their shouts of celebration as
One by one, they finished the course.

But me? I felt no laughter
Bursting from within,
No! Recalling many times of being
Lost on the highway, only panic set in.

Little did I know of one
Standing in a perch center
Of the field ready to shout directions
To those unable to find their way.

This maze of life—
Maze of faith—
So quickly it eludes me,
Leaves me in a state of panic.

But you, O God,
You shout from your perch,
You call my name,
And show me the way.

Thankful

Always someone . . .

Smarter,
Richer,
Faster.

But should there be
A measure for thankfulness,
May there be
No person
More thankful . . .

Than I.